Electrostar
Capital Commuter

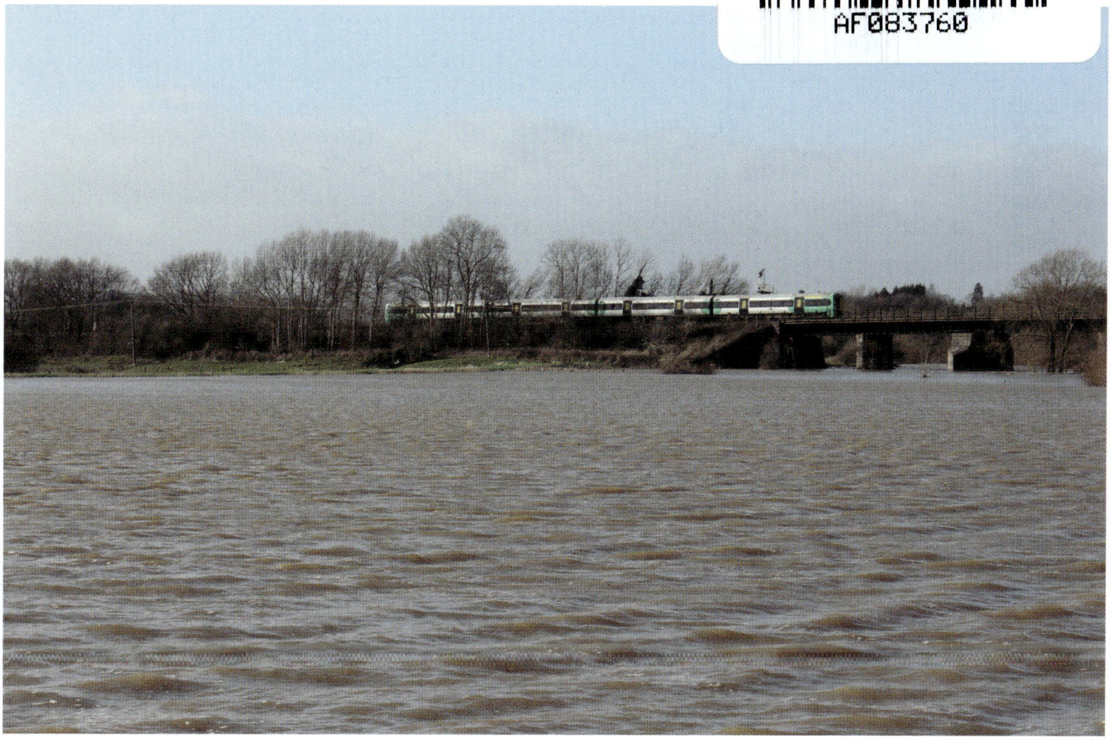

IAN BUCK

KEY Books

BRITAIN'S RAILWAYS SERIES, VOLUME 48

Front cover image: Running just south of Pulborough, near the location of the former Hardham Junction, 377443 is seen in perfect Sussex countryside working an Arun Valley to Victoria service on 8 May 2008.

Title page image: A Class 377 unit passes over the flooded River Arun at Pulborough on 1 February 2014.

Contents page image: Gatwick Express 387206 crosses the Ouse Valley Viaduct on 1 June 2020 with a Brighton to Victoria train.

Back cover image: During a golden sunset, an unidentified Class 377 arrives at Barnham on a train from Bognor Regis on 20 October 2010.

Published by Key Books
An imprint of Key Publishing Ltd
PO Box 100
Stamford
Lincs PE9 1XQ

www.keypublishing.com

The right of Ian Buck to be identified as the author of this book has been asserted in accordance with the Copyright, Designs and Patents Act 1988 Sections 77 and 78.

Copyright © Ian Buck, 2023

ISBN 978 1 80282 669 2

All rights reserved. Reproduction in whole or in part in any form whatsoever or by any means is strictly prohibited without the prior permission of the Publisher.

Typeset by SJmagic DESIGN SERVICES, India.

Contents

Introduction		4
Chapter 1	Class 357s: Southend Line Modernisation	6
Chapter 2	Class 375s: South Eastern Main Line	11
Chapter 3	Class 377: Southern Variety	33
Chapter 4	Class 376s: South Eastern Suburban	59
Chapter 5	Class 378s: Overground Capitalstar	63
Chapter 6	Class 377 and 387s: Through the Thameslink Core	70
Chapter 7	Class 387/1s and Class 387/3s: Great Northern	75
Chapter 8	Class 387/1s: Great Western	80
Chapter 9	Airport Express: Electrostars to Gatwick, Stansted and Heathrow	84
	Class 387/2: Gatwick Express	84
	Class 379: Stansted Express	87
	Class 387/1a: Heathrow Express	90
Chapter 10	Off the Beaten Track	92
Chapter 11	The Future	95

Introduction

During the privatisation of the railway system in the mid-to-late 1990s, most of the longer-distance commuter routes in London and the South East were still operated by slam-door Mark 1-based rolling stock from the 1960s. Network South East, under the indomitable leadership of Chris Green, had started to make inroads into the replacement of slam-door stock with the introduction of Networkers – Class 442s and Class 319s – on the Thameslink route, but uncertainty over the direction the railway was taking and lack of funding brought the process to a halt.

The post-privatisation moratorium on rolling stock orders hit the two biggest suppliers, Alstom and Bombardier, hard and allowed space for Siemens to compete in the same market. The formation of the train-leasing companies and the requirements of franchise agreements got things moving again, with Alstom being 'first off the block' with its Juniper product in the late 1990s. However, apart from a few units for South West Trains, Gatwick Express and Scotrail, this did not prove to be a great success for the company. Then came Siemens with its successful Desiro platform, which achieved sales speculatively at first and then in great numbers from operators around the country.

Not wanting to miss out, Bombardier offered its Electrostar platform. This was a logical follow on from the company's recently introduced Turbostar family of diesel multiple units, which became classes 168, 170 and 171. Of a modular construction, a large number of these units were subsequently built for a number of operators, interestingly concentrated exclusively around the London and South East areas.

To passengers used to draughty and basic slam-door stock with indifferent riding quality, the Electrostars, with their sliding doors, bright interiors, air-sprung suspension and air conditioning, were an enormous step change. This was also the case for the drivers and maintenance staff, who had to learn new skills and techniques. What is possibly most surprising is that the Electrostar platform kept Bombardier's Derby Litchurch Lane production line busy for 18 years, producing 2,085 vehicles between 1999 and 2017, including 96 vehicles for the South African Gautrain. The Electrostar concept was continuously developed during this time but, certainly in appearance, was broadly similar throughout.

In my long career in the railway industry, I have never worked professionally with the Electrostars, although I have spent a great deal of time commuting and travelling for pleasure on them – living in Surrey, it is hard not to! My interest in the units has grown, but I have to confess I was remiss in not photographing units on C2C and Greater Anglia routes as much as I could have. In the past, my Electrostar photography had been incidental to other subjects, but I am now finding myself deliberately hunting these units down, especially as withdrawals, albeit limited, have already started to occur and newer designs are on the horizon.

This book is intended to illustrate the different types of units in the Electrostar family and the lines and areas on which they undertake their reliable day-to-day service to the hundreds of thousands of people who travel around London and the South East every day. In fact, Electrostars have operated regularly into every London termini at some time or other except un-electrified Marylebone and Siemens Desiro-obsessed Waterloo!

Introduction

The following vehicle type codes have been used throughout:

DMOS	Driving Motor Open Standard
MOS	Motor Open Standard
MOSL	Motor Open Standard Lavatory
PTOS	Pantograph Trailer Open Standard
PTOSL	Pantograph Trailer Open Standard Lavatory
DMOC	Driving Motor Open Composite
TOS	Trailer Open Standard
TOSL	Trailer Open Standard Lavatory
PTOSL	Pantograph Trailer Open Standard Lavatory
MOCL	Motor Open Composite Lavatory

377206 is seen just north of Merstham station on May 2008.

Chapter 1
Class 357s Southend Line Modernisation

Class 357/0   357001–357046
Class 357/2   357201–357228
Class 357/3   357312–357328 (converted from 357212–357228 in 2015/16).

All: DMOS-MOS-PTSO-DMOS   25Kv ac

Franchise History

- With Prism Rail from 1997
- With National Express from September 2000
- With Trenitalia from February 2017

Regular Routes

London Fenchurch Street – Shoeburyness via Upminster
London Fenchurch Street – Shoeburyness via Tilbury
London Fenchurch Street – Grays via Upminster

The Class 357s were the first of the Electrostars to enter service and have an uncanny resemblance to the Turbostar Class 170s introduced shortly before. The Class 357s have always been associated with the London Tilbury and Southend routes from Fenchurch Street to Shoeburyness and are based and maintained at East Ham depot.

They are still operating on their designated route since being introduced into service between 1999 and 2002. After initial teething problems, the units have proven to be very reliable. There have been two big changes to the fleet since introduction: the first was the fitting of regenerative braking from 2007, and an internal refurbishment to some of the class from 2015, which created the sub class 357/3.

357217 approaches London's Fenchurch Street passing Shadwell on 26 February 2008. It is seen from the Docklands Light Railway, which parallels the London, Tilbury and Southend (LT&S) line at this point. It carries the earlier blue livery.

357201 at Benfleet on a rainy 29 January 2014. This station serves Canvey Island, a large community on the north shore of the Thames Estuary.

357038 passes along the Thames Estuary as it nears Chalkwell on a service from Shoeburyness to Fenchurch Street on 12 February 2014.

357209 in the heart of London's East End at Fenchurch Street, leaving for Essex on 18 February 2014.

In National Express white livery with C2C branding, 357022 has arrived at Pitsea with a train from Fenchurch Street to Shoeburyness via Upminster on 14 March 2014. This is the junction with the route from Barking via Tilbury, the platform for which is behind the photographer. This was the original route before the cut off via Upminster was opened in 1886.

357003 enters Westcliff-on-Sea on 24 April 2014, on a service from Fenchurch Street to Shoeburyness.

Right: 357216 at Southend Central on 24 April 2014, working from Fenchurch Street to Shoeburyness. This is one of three stations in Southend: Southend East is on the same line and Southend Victoria is on the former Great Eastern Railway route from Liverpool Street. All are still open.

Below: 357327 at Plaistow on 28 December 2018. On the left are the tracks of the London Underground's District Line, which parallel the LT&S route between Bromley by Bow and Upminster. Plaistow was the location for the steam shed for the line prior to electrification.

Above: 357010 at Upminster on 27 November 2015, working from Fenchurch Street to Grays. On the right, the platforms where the District Line trains terminate can be seen, this being the furthest east that they go.

Left: Class 357/0 interior showing the suburban 3+2 seating layout.

Nameplate of 357003.

Chapter 2
Class 375s
South Eastern Main Line

Regular Routes
All South Eastern mainline routes from Victoria, Blackfriars, Charing Cross and Cannon Street to the Kent Coast.
  Medway Valley and Sheerness branches.

Franchise History

- From 13 October 1996, Connex South Eastern
- From June 2003, franchise returned to Strategic Rail Authority
- From 1 April 2006, it became South Eastern Railway* (owned by GOVIA)

* In October 2021, the South Eastern Railway franchise was terminated and became government-run as South Eastern Trains.

The Class 375s were the first of the Electrostar type to be built for a third rail operator and today is the dominant type in use on South Eastern mainline services. They are very different from Class 357s in appearance, primarily because of the corridor connection that set the standard for the rest of the fleets to come. They were originally fitted with Tightlock mechanical couplers, which have since been exchanged for the Dellner type. Between 2015 and 2018, the complete fleet received a refurbishment, which meant, in some cases, internal changes. From December 2022, all trains on South Eastern Railway no longer carry First Class, which will mean the removal of First Class branding and seating from these units in time.

Class 375/3s

375301–375310   DMOC-TOSL-DMOS   Single voltage 750V dc

This sub-class was delivered in 2001 to Connex South Eastern. Upon delivery, 375311–375338 were sent to Connex South Central where they were renumbered 377301–377328 and are now operated as Class 377/3s by Southern. The ten remaining units were put into general use on South Eastern services, settling down on branch line services such as the Medway Valley line, London Bridge to Tunbridge Wells via Redhill and Tonbridge, and eventually taking over the Sheerness branch from the Class 466s.

375305 at Redhill on a London Bridge to Tunbridge Wells service on 30 December 2005. These units have been synonymous with this route since the replacement of slam-door stock in 2004. Since operation was taken over by Southern (with mostly South Eastern crews), they are operated by their 377/3 cousins.

375303 leaving Merstham Tunnel on a London Bridge to Tunbridge Wells service on 30 May 2008. Although forming part of the London to Brighton Main Line, this part of the route was operated by the original South Eastern Railway as far as Redhill, and until being cut back to Redhill these trains formed a sort of residual throwback to that time. South Eastern now no longer operates trains on this route on a daily timetable, although diversions as the result of engineering work are often seen coming this way.

Poking out of the back of the Grosvenor Road Car Sheds near Victoria, 375309 can be seen berthed between peaks on 19 June 2008.

On the Medway Valley, 375310 calls at Maidstone West on 26 February 2014. This is another route regularly worked by Class 375/3s, and between Maidstone West and Paddock Wood is particularly rural and scenic as it follows the River Medway for the most part. This unit is in the earlier white South Eastern livery prior to refurbishment in 2015/16.

Working on the Chatham Main Line, 375302 is seen on the front of a Victoria to Ramsgate train at Rochester's new and relocated station on 22 October 2018. This unit is now in the dark blue livery applied to units that have been through the refurbishment programme. It also shows very distinct First Class branding, which has now become superfluous since December 2022.

375309 comes to a halt at the wonderful South Eastern Railway station at Yalding on the Medway Valley line on 24 July 2020. This photo is very poignant for me, as it represents the memory of the first trip I took to photograph trains after the restrictions following the first COVID-19 lockdown were eased. It seemed, at the time, that we would never be allowed out again! This station, in common with many South Eastern Railway country stations, has staggered platforms.

375306 on the Strood via Maidstone West and the Medway Valley service at Paddock Wood on 28 May 2021. Most of the trains on this line now originate or terminate at Tonbridge, which has far better connections to and from London.

Class 375/6s

375601–375630   DMOC-PTOSL-MOSL-DMOC (original)   Dual voltage 750V dc & 25kV ac
                     DMOS-PTOSL-MOCL-DMOS (refurbished)

This was first Class 375 sub-class to be built in 1999. They were fitted with a dual-voltage capability, which was standard for all electric multiple units (EMUs) at the time. Common sense prevailed, however, as carrying equipment that may never be used proved, unsurprisingly, inefficient. Since 1999, only units working a specific dual-voltage role have had the equipment installed. However, all subsequent Electrostars have been built with space for dual-voltage equipment if it is ever found to be necessary in the future. The interior has a 2+2 seating layout.

Right: 375628 leaves Sittingbourne on 15 July 2010, heading for Victoria.

Below: 375603 at Dover Priory on 26 January 2014. The train on the right is a Hitachi Javelin unit about to set off to St. Pancras via Deal and Ramsgate and the High Speed line. These services took over many of the fast services previously worked by Class 375s.

375604 at Ramsgate depot on 26 February 2014. This is where the South Eastern Electrostar fleet is maintained, and the depot itself has been subject to extensive modification to facilitate this.

375616 heading for the washer at Ramsgate depot on 26 February 2014.

375602 at Nutfield on 26 April 2018, working the daily crew familiarisation run to London Bridge or Selhurst via Redhill and back. These runs ensure drivers retain knowledge of this route for diversionary purposes.

375614 entering Tonbridge Jubilee Sidings on 11 September 2020. This is one of the many berthing points around the South Eastern routes that fill up outside of the morning and evening peaks.

375612 at Minster on 24 September 2021. Just past this station is the junction with the line from Dover via Deal to Ramsgate. The lines in the Thanet area of Kent were complicated owing to the presence of two rival companies, the South Eastern Railway and London, Chatham and Dover Railway (LC&DR), each with their own lines serving Margate and Ramsgate. However, the Southern Railway sorted out the mess in the 1920s, giving us the network we have today.

375630 at Dunton Green on 2 July 2022, working a Charing Cross-bound train. This line was opened in 1868 and provided a quicker route than the original one via Redhill, which in turn became very secondary in nature.

Class 375s

Class 375/7s

375701–375715   DMOC-TOSL-MOSL-DMOC   (original)   Single voltage 750V dc
                  DMOS-TOSL-MOCL-DMOS   (refurbished)

Another small batch of units, but this time for dc operation only. All of this sub-class has now been refurbished, with some changes to the designation of the unit formation. The units entered service in 2000, and the whole 375 fleet was refurbished between 2015 and 2018 but not in number or sub-class order.

Above: 375703 at Wandsworth Road on 20 January 2006. Today, this scene has changed beyond all recognition. The gasometer has gone, and there has been massive high-rise housing development; the iconic Battersea Power Station, however, remains.

Right: 375715 at Canterbury West on 15 July 2010 on a Ramsgate to Charing Cross via Ashford and Tonbridge service. To the far left of the picture the overhead signalbox can be glimpsed, which remains in situ despite no longer being of use. The gap in the middle of the tracks is where a couple of through roads were once located, now long disused and lifted.

357715 at Otford on a Ramsgate via Maidstone East and Ashford International service on 2 May 2014. The unit is in the white South Eastern livery used before the units were refurbished.

375710 at Waterloo East on 20 May 2014. This is the first stop out of Charing Cross, and all trains stop here to give interchange with the "other" Waterloo. They also now all stop at the next station, London Bridge, to give further interchange with Thameslink.

With the imposing station building of Chatham behind, 375709 pauses on its way to Victoria on 22 October 2018. Once a major Royal Navy base, Chatham is one of a string of closely spaced towns and cities along the River Medway, along with Gillingham, Rochester, Strood and Maidstone, which together make up the Medway Towns.

Seen from the Linton Road bridge, 375706 is commencing its run to Charing Cross via Tonbridge on 18 December 2020. Hastings has quite frequent services to London, with three per hour including one operated by Southern to Victoria via Eastbourne.

375707 passes Frant while working a Hastings semi-fast service on 10 December 2021. This route was famous for its narrow tunnels, which required restricted-width steam coaches and diesel units. To allow standard electric units, the line was singled through the tunnels, gaining stock flexibility at the cost of operational flexibility.

375707 is seen passing down the centre road at Redhill, on 11 July 2022. This is a regular daily empty stock move between Tonbridge and Selhurst Depot/London Bridge designed to maintain South Eastern route knowledge.

Class 375/8s

375801–375830   DMOC-TOSL-MOSL-DMOC   (original)   Single voltage 750V dc
                 DMOS-TOSL-MOCL-DMOS   (refurbished)

Yet another small batch of units, but this time carrying on the incremental increase in the fleet. All of this sub-class has now been refurbished, with some changes to the designation of the unit formation.

Right: 375801 thunders through Shortlands on 26 October 2005.

Below: With the iconic Battersea Power Station in the background, 375819 enters the car sheds at Grosvenor Road on 16 January 2006. These sheds are used for berthing and cleaning trains outside and in between the peaks. The steepness of the grade out of Victoria can be seen as the line climbs to cross the Thames.

375813 calls at Canterbury East on 15 July 2010. In common with many large towns in Kent, Canterbury has two stations. The Southern Railway undertook a fair amount of rationalisation but here, as at Maidstone and Bromley, the old way remains. This station lies on the former LC&DR route from Faversham to Dover. Canterbury West is on the South Eastern route from Ashford to Ramsgate.

375818 calls at Waterloo East on 20 May 2014. It is not to be confused with the far larger South Western terminus next door, which is reached by a long walk over the footbridge seen in the distance. Waterloo East has the privilege of being served by two Underground stations on the same line, accessed at each end of the station – Waterloo and Southwark on the Jubilee Line.

On a diverted Charing Cross to Hastings service, 375803 hammers through Nutfield on 7 May 2018. Hastings trains are usually diverted this way when engineering works close the direct route north of Tonbridge.

The bright sunshine showing off its South Eastern blue livery to fine aplomb, 375825 calls at Rochester on its way to the Thanet Coast on 22 October 2018.

Seemingly running through a green tunnel, the sort of which make rail photography very difficult, 375830 is actually deep in urban Tunbridge Wells as it leaves High Brooms for Hastings on 27 August 2020.

375829 is seen leaving Bletchingley Tunnel and making its way to Redhill on a diverted train from Hastings on 29 August 2021.

Class 375s

Class 375/9s

375901–375927   DMOC-TOSL-MOSL-DMOC   Single voltage 750V dc

This sub-class were the last of the fleet of Class 375s to be built, being finished in 2003. These differed from the rest in having 3+2 suburban-type seating in Standard Class. All of this sub-class have now been refurbished.

Above: 375918 at Bromley South on 26 August 2005.

Right: 375922 at Nutfield on 24 January 2009 on yet another diverted Hastings line train. The people on the platform were not waiting for the Electrostar – a few minutes later Bulleid Battle of Britain Pacific 34067 *Tangmere* thundered through on a railtour.

375913 at St Leonards Warrior Square on 11 April 2009. This station unusually lies squeezed in between two tunnels, and the train is seen from atop the mouth of the tunnel at the Hastings end.

375915 at Ramsgate on 26 February 2014, making a shunt move through the carriage washer at the depot. Although there are a number of depots and cleaning sheds scattered around the South Eastern line, all of the Class 375 Electrostars call Ramsgate home.

375921 pauses at Sevenoaks on 2 May 2014, whilst working from Charing Cross to the Kent coast.

375911 passing Knockholt on 16 September 2022. Trains are really flying at this point!

Interior of a Class 375/9 showing the 3+2 suburban seat layout.

Left: 375920 arriving at Headcorn on 3 October 2020. The train is taking the platform road, as it is forming a stopping service from Dover to Charing Cross. The centre roads are hardly used by passenger trains since the opening of the High Speed 1 route meant the diversion of all fast trains from Ashford to terminate at St. Pancras International.

Below: 375905 arriving at Hastings on 18 March 2022. It has just passed through the tunnel that stretches almost the complete distance from St Leonards Warrior Square, which can just be glimpsed through the tunnel. The Linton Road bridge, which gives a panoramic view of operations at Hastings, can be seen above the train.

Class 377/5s

377501–377523   DMOC-MOSL-PTOSL-DMOC   Dual voltage 750V dc & 25kV ac

Regular Routes
Victoria/Blackfriars to Ramsgate via Maidstone East and Ashford International.
The introduction of the Class 377/5s and their service with Thameslink is documented in Chapter 6, but as they are included in the current South Eastern fleet, this part of their life is described here.

After the somewhat belated introduction of Class 700 units on to the Thameslink services, the 377/5 sub-class became surplus to requirement. However, South Eastern required more units, so the class was transferred to that franchise but continued to be maintained at Selhurst depot. The transfer took place in two stages, during 2016 and 2017.

Currently, there are plans for them to be transferred to Southern, but this is dependent on more Class 707s being transferred to South Eastern, which in turn is dependent on Class 710s coming into operation on South Western – confusing!

377515 passes through Eynsford on the Darent Valley line as it heads towards Ramsgate via Maidstone East on 4 July 2020. This line was opened by the LC&DR, the station building of which can be seen on the right. Class 377/5s are mostly used on this route, but not exclusively, and can turn up elsewhere.

377508 passing underneath the South London line at Brixton with a train from Victoria to Ramsgate via the Medway towns on 24 April 2021.

Unusually seen on the Hastings line, 377523 speeds through Frant as it heads for the coast on 15 May 2021.

377513 disappears east after passing through Shortlands with a Victoria to Ashford International via Maidstone East train on 27 September 2021.

Chapter 3

Class 377 Southern Variety

Regular Routes

All electrified routes operated by Southern, with extensions to Southampton on South Western Railway and Watford Junction on the West Coast Main Line (WCML). Since the withdrawal of Class 455 EMUs in May 2022, Class 377s have become the dominant Southern unit.

Franchise History

- On 26 May 1996: Connex South Central commenced operation of the Network South Central Franchise.
- 26 August 2001: Govia took over the franchise, trading as SouthCentral.
- May 2003: the franchise was rebranded as Southern.
- December 2008: Gatwick Express was merged into the SouthCentral franchise.
- July 2015: the SouthCentral franchise was merged with Thameslink and Great Northern to be known as Govia Thameslink Railway. The Southern brand was retained.

The Southern Electrostar fleet is large and surprisingly mixed and varied. The first units were introduced into service in 2003, following a massive power supply upgrade programme on the Southern system. With their air conditioning and power-operated doors, they consumed far more power than the units the slam-door Mark 1 stock that they replaced. They were also fitted with Dellner couplers, which at the time made them unique.

Since the withdrawal of Class 455s in May 2022, Southern has become almost an entirely Class 377-operated railway: the only exceptions are a few Class 313s, which are expected to be gone by May 2023, and the diesel Turbostars, which operate the Uckfield and Ashford to Hastings services.

Southern have been undertaking a refurbishment project called 'Project Aurora', which commenced in 2021. It is intended to cover all Class 377s and will be completed in 2025.

Class 377/1s

377101–377164   DMOC-MOSL-PTOSL-DMOC   Single voltage 750V dc

Working a Horsham to Victoria local service, 377111 halts at Earlswood on 29 December 2005. Earlswood retains some of its early 20th century charm.

In the heart of 'commuterland', 377133 arrives at Clapham Junction on a service from the south coast on 3 July 2014. Since the withdrawal of Class 455s in May 2022, all calls by Southern trains are Electrostars.

In the heart of the Arun Valley, 377109 arrives at Amberley with a Horsham to Bognor Regis stopping train. This would have formed the rear of a train from Victoria to Southampton or Portsmouth Harbour, which would have detached at Horsham and the front portion would have passed through Amberley non-stop about ten minutes earlier.

At Horsham, trains for the Arun Valley split and join, arriving as an eight car and heading south first as a four-car fast service to Barnham, then Portsmouth or Southampton, closely followed by the rear four as a stopping train to Bognor Regis. The reverse happens in the opposite direction. On 24 March 2018, 377158 awaits to depart for Victoria.

Blending in with the South Downs, and with the local bovine population seemingly not interested, 377103 approaches Arundel on 29 September 2018.

In South Western territory, 377102 is working a Brighton to Portsmouth Harbour train into the small halt at Hilsea on 13 March 2020.

On 30 July 2020, 377135 is seen in the deep cutting near Merstham on the Quarry Line, working a southbound coastal service. This route was built by the London, Brighton and South Coast Railway to avoid Redhill and capacity problems with the South Eastern Railway, effectively quadrupling the Brighton Main Line. As such, it is one of the fastest sections on the route.

Above: 377142 leaves the famous north portal of Clayton Tunnel on 17 August 2020. The castellated tunnel mouth was constructed in 1841 to allegedly "reassure" passengers fearful about entering a long railway tunnel for the first time. Interestingly, the south portal is plain, as were the tunnel mouths on the three previous tunnels on the route and the one after!

Right: 377147 passes Pevensey Bay at speed on 21 January 2022, working an Ore to Victoria service that will join with another unit at Eastbourne. Pevensey Bay has the least level of service on the Southern network, being served by only a handful of trains on weekdays.

On a train for the South Coast from Victoria, 377152 hurtles past Salfords on the mainline on 24 March 2022. Salfords is my local station and was the last to be opened on the Brighton line and has only ever had platforms on the slow lines.

Electrostar: Capital Commuter

Class 377/2s

377201–377215   DMOC-MOSL-PTOSL-DMOC   Dual voltage 750V dc & 25kV ac

This small class of 15 units is a special breed, as it is the only subclass of the original 377 fleet to be dual voltage. They are fitted with pantographs for working under 25kv AC wires as well as on the third rail. This was primarily so that they could work services north from Clapham Junction on the WCML as far as Milton Keynes Central. This route has been subject to a number of alterations and changes over the years, with even Siemens Desiro Class 350/3s from the London Midland route working for a short period. Economies made following COVID-19 have meant the service now terminates at Watford Junction, with most trains starting from East Croydon. Following a long period of Class 377/7 operation, 377/2 has resumed its role as the prime class on this service, mostly operating as single units. As only a handful of units are required for Watford Junction, those not allocated can turn up almost anywhere on the Southern network.

377209 is at Lingfield on a train from Victoria to East Grinstead on 22 September 2005. At this time, those units not working the West London line seemed to turn up often on the Oxted line. Lingfield is famous for its racecourse, which is only a short walk away. Long gone are the days of race specials, however, some of which used to include Pullman cars.

377210 at West Brompton on 21 February 2007. On its intended route, the unit is operating between Milton Keynes Central and Gatwick Airport. This scene has changed beyond all recognition since this image was taken, however, as the Earls Court Exhibition Centre behind the station has been closed and demolished. This must have taken a lot of passenger potential away from this station, but there is strong interchange with the District Line and the proposed new housing in the area will surely have a positive effect on passenger numbers.

377212 at Watford Junction on 21 June 2007. At this time, most of the Southern Electrostars heading up the West Coast Main Line terminated at Milton Keynes Central, but one per day terminated at the bay platform 9 at Watford Junction. Note the raised pantograph. Power changeover to third rail occurs at North Pole Junction on the West London Line. Nowadays, virtually all Southern trains via the West London Line terminate at Watford Junction.

377208 arrives at Tadworth on the last day of 2013. One has to question the use of such a long train on a fairly lightly used route such as the Purley to Tattenham Corner line?

377213 flying through Aldrington on 17 April 2018. This has got to be the most uninviting station on the East Coastway route, with narrow platforms and high palisade fencing giving it a claustrophobic prison-like ambience.

377206 entering the centre turnback siding at West Croydon on 19 November 2020. This train would have come down from Victoria and run via Streatham Hill and Crystal Palace to terminate at West Croydon, where it would reverse and retrace its steps to Victoria. This siding was installed after the commencement of Overground services to West Croydon, which now use the bay platform.

Heading for East Croydon on the somewhat truncated service currently operated from Watford Junction, 377209 is seen at Kensington Olympia on 4 October 2022. The usefulness of this service has been dented by the frequent Overground service on this route and lack of WCML connections at Watford Junction.

With its headlight burning bright on a dismal winter's day, 377204 arrives at Chipstead on the Tattenham Corner branch heading for London Bridge on 31 January 2013.

Class 377/3

377301–377328   DMOC-PTOSL-DMOS   Single voltage 750V dc only

These are the original Class 377s, and the 28 units in this sub-class have operated a number of services around Southern. As new units in 2001/2002, they started on mainline duties particularly on the flagship Victoria to Brighton fast services. After the introduction of more four-car units, the 377s gravitated to lesser-used routes, running local services on the Coastway lines. The introduction of Class 313s and an increase in passenger numbers meant their replacement and being sent to strengthen Metro services in South London. After the introduction of five-car 377 units, however, they became more commonly used again, being seen on the Oxted Line. Throughout all of these changes, the route between Redhill and Tonbridge has remained a staple.

Left: 377317 passes Gatwick Airport on 27 March 2007 with another 317/3 leading. At this time, it was common to see trains such as this operating the fast Brighton to Victoria route, which at this point did not stop at Gatwick Airport. The history of the Brighton fast trains goes back a long time. The 1933 electrification introduced non-stop trains on the hour, every hour. Over the years, stops were added at East Croydon and Clapham Junction with little change in journey time. In 2022, the Brighton fast service forms part of the Gatwick Express route using Class 387/2s, only stopping at Gatwick Airport on their way to Brighton.

Below: Off the beaten track, 377307 speeds through Ockley on a diverted Brighton to Victoria via Horsham service on 28 December 2006. This route forms part of the Mid Sussex line, but in the era of the Electrostar it sees very few fast mainline trains aside from diversions.

Lost in the shingle wasteland at Tide Mills, 377325 approaches Bishopstone while working a Brighton to Seaford train on 1 June 2009. Class 377/3s were quite common on this route until supplanted by Class 313s later in 2009. The tables are turning, however, as the Class 313s are to be replaced by Class 377s early in 2023.

Two Class 377/3 units form a South London Metro service from Epsom to Victoria approaching Mitcham Junction with 377324 leading on 7 March 2014. The landscape of Mitcham Common can give quite a desolate appearance, despite being deep within the South London suburbs. At Mitcham Junction, this line makes good connection with the Croydon Tramlink system.

377305 approaching West Croydon on 19 August 2015. This is a nine-car train made up of three Class 377/3 units probably working from Epsom to London Bridge or Victoria. Seen to the left of the picture is part of the Croydon tram system, which rises up to cross the Sutton to West Croydon line at about the same place where the junction for the Wimbledon line was prior to 1997.

377327 passing Earlswood in the snow on 6 January 2010. The train is departing the Quarry Line, which bypasses Redhill and is normally used by all Brighton Line fast trains.

Above: A three-car unit was formed out of 377442 whilst the MOSL 788442 was repaired following damage. This was renumbered 377342 and is seen at Brighton on a Coastway East service on 9 March 2020.

Right: During and post pandemic, the off-peak service to East Grinstead was reduced to hourly runs, but the trains were made longer. This has meant all sorts of unusual lengths, including three, four and sometimes five-car 377s. Here, an 11-car train arrives at East Grinstead, led by 377323, on 22 October 2020.

Working a service that has become a staple for this sub-class, 377309 arrives at Godstone from Redhill on 22 April 2022 and will proceed on to Tonbridge.

Class 377/4s

377401–377475   DMOC-MOSL-PTOSL-DMOC   Single voltage 750V dc

The 75 units of this sub-class, together with the Class 377/1s, form the backbone of Southern's mainline fleet. The units are maintained at Selhurst and Brighton depots, and along with the other 377 sub classes, are seen almost anywhere on the Southern network.

377459 at Southease on 17 September 2005. Currently, 377s are only seen on the Seaford branch on the few peak through trains from Victoria and when covering for Class 313s. This will change in 2023, however, when it is planned to withdraw Class 313 units. The Seaford branch is interesting in having a large freight presence and an eclectic mix of downland, industrial and coastal scenery in its short length. Southease is almost totally isolated, with just a farm and a youth hostel nearby, but it still has an hourly service.

377407 is passing through the small station of Hilsea in the Portsmouth suburbs with a train for Portsmouth Harbour on 15 July 2009. This is one of the few locations where Electrostars rub shoulders with their Siemens Desiro competitors, as South Western Railway use them on its trains from Portsmouth to London and Southampton.

Running just south of Pulborough, near the location of the former Hardham Junction, 377443 is seen in perfect Sussex countryside working an Arun Valley to Victoria service on 8 May 2008.

377425 at Barnham on 28 August 2006. Barnham is a very busy station, as it is the junction for Bognor Regis and the Arun Valley line. A certain amount of joining and splitting is still undertaken here.

377408 and 377440 under the famous roof of Brighton station on 10 February 2007. Brighton has a massive and well-used station, as is befitting for a city. The platforms seen here, 1, 2 and 3, serve the West Coastway trains in the direction of Worthing and Portsmouth. The only connection between these routes and the mainlines is the set of points on platform 3 in the foreground, and these only allow a four-car unit!

377444 near Ifield on 10 April 2007. This station is situated in the western suburbs of Crawley and is surprisingly busy for its size, although these days Crawley and Horsham have almost joined together, thanks to ever more new housing being built. Arun Valley Electrostars pass here every 30 minutes, running fast from Horsham to Crawley.

Normans Bay is a small halt by the sea between Eastbourne and Hastings that sees an hourly service. On 2 April 2018, 377420 speeds past on the Ore section of a train from Victoria.

377471 is arriving at Ore to form a train to Victoria on 5 September 2020. This is the end of the electrification from Eastbourne, which actually ends just past the crossover in the distance, allowing trains to reverse here rather than congested Hastings. Carriage sidings and a cleaning shed used to be located to the left of the photo but are now no more.

Above: 377410 at Reigate on 11 September 2021. Reigate is the first station on the Guildford line from Redhill, and electrification reached here in 1932. Today's basic service is twice per hour to and from Victoria, however, the length of Reigate's platform only allows four-car units. In peaks, this means that Reigate portions are still attached and detached at Redhill, in the same manner that they have been for 90 years.

Left: 377472 was one of two units (alongside 377474) that took part in a bid to break the London to Brighton speed record on 11 September 2005. The attempt was successful, and the record now stands at just under 37 minutes. To commemorate the occasion, the units received celebratory vinyls.

377423 approaching on the Mole Valley route near Ashtead on a sunny 16 June 2022. Coming from Horsham via Dorking, this train will now proceed to Victoria via Epsom and Sutton. This sub-class is not seen so much on this route these days, being now mostly the preserve of classes 377/6 and 377/7.

377414 arriving at Glynde, in the heart of the South Downs, on 12 September 2022 with a Brighton to Hastings train. Normal quiet, rural Glynde comes to life in the summer as it is close to the famous Glyndebourne Opera Festival.

A class 377/4 crosses the River Ouse at Southerham Junction on 21 April 2021. Just to the right of the bridge is the junction for the Newhaven and Seaford branch. This train will be running on at least as far as Eastbourne.

Class 377/6s

377601–377628   DMOC-MOSL-TOSL-MOS(2)-DMOS   Single voltage 750V dc

In order to cover more diagrams following a boom in passenger numbers, in 2012, Southern decided to order further batches of Electrostar units. This time, the units were to be of a five-car formation and have a window layout similar to Class 379 and the later Class 387 units. Following COVID-19 and the resultant drop in passenger numbers, the five-car formation has proved useful in replacing the eight-car Class 455 formations.

Although part of the Class 377 pool, the 377/6s are most often seen working Victoria to Horsham via Dorking and South London Metro trains and played a big part in the demise of Class 455s in 2022, in conjunction with their Class 377/7 cousins.

377625 arriving at Dorking 31 December 2013. The signalbox on the left is one of the last operating Southern Railway 'Glasshouse' types still in operation. Dorking is served by both Southern services from Victoria and South Western services from Waterloo. Note the SWR class 455 on the right of the photo.

Although in theory a suburban unit, the seating layout is 2+2 with a number of tables scattered about. Unfortunately the seats are rather hard and high backed giving a claustrophobic ambience and challenging comfort on the longer journeys.

377619 Salfords
29 March 2014. At this time class 377/6 were often seen working fast trains to Brighton especially at weekends.

Right: Arriving at Whyteleafe South on 3 April 2014 is 377613. This unit will be joining with another at Purley that will have used the Chipstead Valley line from Tattenham Corner and the two will then proceed from Purley to London Bridge.

Below: 377610 at Holmwood 21 April 2014. This is a train from Horsham to Victoria and Holmwood is one of the three little used stations between Horsham and Dorking. Even so, it maintains a basic hourly service throughout the day.

Another Brighton Line weekend working sees 377605 departing Balcombe and heading for Victoria on 26 May 2014.

Left: 377609 South Croydon 25 August 2017 working a London Bridge to Caterham service. The unit is running on the fifth reversible line between East Croydon and South Croydon. Just south of this station the Oxted lines to East Grinstead and Uckfield branch off.

Below: The Chipstead Valley route was constructed at the beginning of the 20th century by the South Eastern & Chatham Railway with the prime objective of syphoning off some of the lucrative Derby Day traffic at Epsom Downs Racecourse. The topography of the Surrey Hills meant a curvaceous and heavily graded line, which was ideal for electrification. The Southern Railway did this in 1928 in order to try and attract more passengers. 377625 curves its way into Coulsdon Town station on a train from Tattenham Corner on 30 October 2021.

377625 catches a patch of sun at Warnham on 19 November 2022. Yet another signal failure had decimated the service and the sun was dropping rapidly as the train we were waiting for, the Class 73-hauled rail head treatment trains (RHTT), was stuck behind this one.

377614 calls at West Norwood on a London Bridge to Beckenham Junction service on 9 December 2022. I have included this photo out of sheer indulgence as it was the last Class 377 that I had managed to take a photo of.

Class 377/7s

377701–377708   DMOC-MOSL-PTOSL-MOS(2)-DMOS   Dual voltage 750V dc & 25kV ac

This small sub-class of only eight units was the last order by Southern for Electrostars, being delivered in 2014. Their dual-voltage capability was designed to allow them to work on the Southern services on the West London line, however, after spending some time on these services, the downturn following COVID-19 and the withdrawal of Class 455s saw them being more gainfully employed with their class 377/6 cousins.

Left: 377706 Clapham Junction on 30 July 2014 with an evening peak service heading for the Mole Valley. Clapham Junction retains its status as one of the busiest railway locations in the world. There is hardly a moment when a train is not stopped or moving through the station.

Below: 377703 at Watford Junction on 30 July 2014. This was the service that these units were originally built for, replacing the four-car 377/2 units previously used. Post-pandemic cut backs meant they were replaced with class 377/2 and their five-car formation being more usefully employed on Metro services to replace nine-car class 455 trains.

377704 has reached the end of the line at Caterham on a dark and wet 11 December 2020. This is the terminus of a short but busy branch from Purley, which since the demise of the Class 455, is wholly served by Electrostars.

377705 at Holmwood 27 July 2020. The 377/7 sub class works hand in hand with class 377/6 and is mostly seen working the same duties. The original waiting shelter and, behind the second vehicle, the disused signal box are all that is left of the old station. This line was once considered a mainline with fast trains to Bognor Regis and Portsmouth, but became a secondary route when through services were diverted by the more attractive traffic proposition of Gatwick Airport more than 40 years ago.

Above: 377707 Whyteleafe 27 October 2020. The Caterham branch has suffered a boom and bust with its train service during the life of the Electrostars. The basic service was always two trains per hour but it was increased by Southern to four trains per hour. Then came the pandemic, following which service cuts and the withdrawal of the Class 455s meant it was reduced to half hourly.

Left: 377701 works a London Bridge to Caterham train at Kenley on 9 March 2022. This would have split off from another 377/7 or 377/6 at the previous station, Purley. Just behind the leading vehicle is the original highly gabled station building, which is now used as offices.

377701 at Peckham Rye with an East Croydon to London Bridge via Tulse Hill stopping service on 13 January 2023.

Chapter 4
Class 376s
South Eastern Suburban

376001–376036   DMOS-MOS-TOS-MOS-DMOS   Single voltage 750V dc

This is probably the most basic form of Electrostar. These five-car units were acquired by South Eastern in 2004/2005 for operating short-distance suburban services. There is no air conditioning, ventilation is by hopper lights and there are no toilets. Seating is very basic, some would say harsh, with no First Class. The cab front has no corridor connection and has been designed to be as flat as possible to try and prevent 'train surfing', which was once very prevalent in South East London. The doors are slightly wider than those on classes 375 and 376 to allow faster egress and ingress and are of the 'sliding into pockets' type, which tend to operate faster.

The fleet is based at South Eastern's suburban depot at Slade Green but are often sent to Ramsgate for examination, which is where the Electrostar expertise sits. South Eastern plan to undertake a light refurbishment of these vehicles in 2023, but there will be no air conditioning or toilets fitted.

End of the line at Hayes on what is somewhat confusingly called the Mid-Kent line. 376008 awaits its return to Charing Cross on 5 November 2009. This is one of the few suburban termini south of the river and was opened by the South Eastern Railway in 1882 to tap potential commuter traffic. In 2022, it still manages four trains per hour throughout most of the day.

On just the sort of inner-suburban service it was designed for, 376032 is seen entering Lewisham on 27 May 2008. Lewisham is a complex junction with many routes joining and separating and has always been a place of great congestion. Its busyness is enhanced by being an interchange with a branch of the Docklands Light Railway.

376020 at a snowy Elmstead Woods on 21 December 2009. This train is heading to Orpington, but Class 376s operate randomly in conjunction with Networker units over most routes emanating from Cannon Street or Charing Cross. However, they cannot work together with the much larger Networker fleet and must keep to their own separate diagrams.

376035 arriving at Woolwich Dockyard on 24 August 2010. This is an interesting station squeezed into an urban area and is a reminder of Woolwich's earlier reliance on the nearby River Thames.

376005 at Slade Green on 15 May 2014. Just to the left of the picture the Slade Green maintenance depot can be glimpsed. This is where the Class 376 units are maintained, along with South Eastern's vast fleet of Networker units.

376030 at Deptford with a North Kent line train to Dartford via Abbey Wood on 20 December 2014. This station is on the original London and Greenwich Railway, which was opened in 1838, making it London's first railway line. It was notable that almost the entire route was carried on a very long viaduct.

376012 halts at Elmstead Woods on 29 June 2022. Lack of investment over the years, followed by more enlightened and sympathetic modernisation, has left the South Eastern suburban network with a number of pleasantly restored stations, of which Elmstead Woods is one.

The very basic interior of Class 376s is shown to good effect here. These are true people movers, more akin to a glorified tube train with no toilet facilities and maximum standing room.

Left: 376003 arrives at London Bridge with a Cannon Street to Cannon Street via the North Kent Line and the Dartford Loop on 9 December 2022.

Below: 376009 arrives at Hither Green working a Charing Cross to Dartford via Sidcup service on 8 February 2023.

Chapter 5
Class 378s Overground Capitalstar

378001–378024	750V dc & 25kV ac
378135–378154	750V dc only
378201–378224	750V dc & 25kV ac (ex-378001–378024 when made four-car)
378225–378234 & 378255-7	750V dc & 25kV ac

Three-car	DMOS-PTOS-DMOS
Four-car	DMOS-MOS-PTOS-DMOS
Five-car	DMOS-MOS-PTOS-MOS-DMOS

Regular Routes

Richmond–Camden Road–Stratford (North London Line)
Clapham Junction–Willesden Junction– Stratford (West London Line)
Clapham Junction–Denmark Hill–Highbury & Islington (South London Line)
West Croydon/Crystal Palace – Highbury & Islington
New Cross–Dalston Junction (East London Line)

Three-car 378001 at Nutfield on test on the Redhill to Tonbridge line on 21 January 2009. Before their introduction into service, the Class 378 units were commissioned by Bombardier in the former Southern Region workshops at Chart Leacon. This meant a number of test runs were undertaken between Ashford and Redhill before they were released into the congested London area.

The success of the London Overground operation can be measured to some extent by the increasing length of the trains that operate on it. Starting with the delivery of the first batch of 24 Overground Capitalstar three-car units in 2009, the next batch were delivered as four-car units, and the continuing increase in patronage led to the fitting of a fifth coach in 2016.

More and more Overground routes have been added, which now cover most of the short-distance local services around London. Not all services are operated by Class 378s, but they do hold the monopoly on what were once known as the North, East, West and South London lines, working very intense services at a frequency only dreamt of 20 years ago. The Class 378/1s, being dc only, operate services over the East London line from West Croydon and Crystal Palace to Dalston Junction. One notable route operated for a short while was from Euston to Watford Junction, bringing Electrostars into yet another London terminal.

Several of the units have received names, as follows:

378135 *Daks Hamilton*
378204 *Professor Sir Peter Hall*
378232 *Jeff Langston*
378136 *Transport for London*
378211 *Gary Hunter*
378233 *Ian Brown CBE*

Left: Three-car 378015 approaching Brondesbury on 1 October 2009. This is the core North London line now operated between Richmond/Clapham Junction to Stratford. On this section of the route, trains run every 5–6 minutes, a far cry from the service in British Rail days when it used to be every 20 minutes.

Below: 378013 at Clapham Junction on 15 August 2009. This is the West London line, which has been improved and expanded significantly since reopening from Clapham Junction to Willesden Junction in 1994. This has been helped by the opening of new stations, a Westfield shopping centre at Shepherd's Bush, new housing development and a very frequent service.

Above: Four-car 378228 calls at West Brompton on the West London Line on 18 February 2014. Class 378s are maintained at New Cross Gate and Willesden Junction depots and are the slowest of the Electrostars, with a maximum speed of 75mph.

Right: 378151 and 378201 at Crystal Palace on 2 May 2014. These two units are seen through the arches of the old station, which was built on a grandiose scale for exhibitions at the old Crystal Palace before it burned down in 1936. The name lives on in the area and in South London's premier football team. The station itself has been sympathetically restored and improved since the advent of the Overground.

378232 at Watford Junction on 30 July 2014. For a short while, prior to the introduction of Class 710 Aventra units in 2019, this route allowed Electrostars to travel to Euston, meaning they have operated to all London terminals except non-electrified Marylebone and Siemens Desiro-monopolised Waterloo!

378146 at Whitechapel on 9 June 2010. Whitechapel is on the East London line and is served by trains for lines to New Cross, West Croydon/Crystal Palace and the South London line. This is also the line that passes through Brunel's famous Thames Tunnel between Wapping and Rotherhithe.

378142 at Anerley on 3 December 2014. This route, and its sister to Crystal Palace, is the normal preserve of the 378/1 dc-only sub class, although 378/2 are not unknown here either.

Another route that sees its fair share of 378/1 units is the South London line, which runs between Clapham Junction and Dalston Junction utilising a reinstated spur connecting with the East London Line at Surrey Quays. 378138 is seen arriving at Peckham Rye on a blustery and wet 13 January 2023.

378231 approaching Willesden Junction High Level on 10 April 2021. This unit is showing the modified livery that is slowly being introduced to the fleet as units become due for maintenance.

Electrostar: Capital Commuter

378221 at Wandsworth Road on 31 July 2021. This is working a train to Highbury & Islington and is just joining the South London line. After Queens Road Peckham, it will join the East London line and later at Shoreditch on the North London line. The Overground almost forms a circle around inner London if you allow for the break at Clapham Junction.

378230 at South Acton on 9 November 2022, working from Richmond to Stratford. I remember using this station in the 1970s, when it was served every 20 minutes by rundown and vandalised slam-door stock to Broad Street with hardly any passengers. Sometimes things do change for the better!

Class 378s

Above left: Class 378 passenger doors share some similarities with Class 376's, in that they consist of sliding doors into pockets. These are considered to be faster in operation, which is useful at the many stops these trains make on their journeys.

Above right: The Capitalstar has longitudinal seating in common with tube trains, as seen in 378151 on 2 May 2014. In a five-car train, there is seating for 272 passengers and standing room for 900 more. Trains are often filled to capacity at all times of the day.

Below: 378222 awaits departure from Richmond on 17 November 2022. It will soon commence its almost one-hour trek across North and East London stopping all stations to Stratford.

Chapter 6

Class 377 and 387s Through the Thameslink Core

Next it was the turn of the Midland Main Line to see the Electrostar. Using a reopened link, new Thameslink services were introduced in 1986 between Southern lines and the Midland Main Line with dual-voltage Class 319 units. Incremental improvements and booming passenger numbers meant more rolling stock was required. By the time the Class 377 and 387 Electrostars arrived on the route, the service had been franchised to the First Group and was branded First Capital Connect; however, in the minds of staff and passengers alike it would always be Thameslink, so this title was tacitly retained. The Class 377/5 units were the first to arrive in 2009, with additional class 387/1 units arriving in 2014.

The Electrostars are seen no more in passenger use on the Thameslink route, with all services now being handled by Siemens Class 700 units, although occasional stock moves between Hornsey and Selhurst can be seen. The 'Core' refers to the centre part of the network between St. Pancras International and Blackfriars, where all the services come together at St. Pancras and separate again at Blackfriars.

Class 377/5s

377501–377523   DMOC-MOSL-PTOSL-DMOC   750V dc & 25kV ac

To accommodate planned improvements to the service, Southern, in a very convoluted lease and stock transfer deal, ordered 23 dual-voltage Electrostars to be known as Class 377/5s. Initially intended to free up Southern Class 319 units for Thameslink, they very quickly became sub-leased to Thameslink

Sparkling new 377505 heads north through Horley on 1 June 2009, demonstrating its third rail capability.

in First Capital Connect livery but with Southern interiors. In another twist to the story, late delivery of these units meant Southern had to lease a number of Class 377/2s to Thameslink, which were covered by borrowed Siemens Desiro Class 350/2 units on the Watford Junction services. This is covered in Chapter 11. To further complicate the story, the 377/5s were then transferred to South Eastern when Thameslink had finished with them (see Chapter 3). The units were maintained by Thameslink in the Bedford Cauldwell depot.

Above: Demonstrating its overhead capability, 377509 is seen at Kentish Town on 7 October 2009 on a southbound service.

Right: 377523 at Bedford on 31 January 2012, having arrived from Brighton. At this time, this was the northern extremity of Thameslink services, which today also include Cambridge and Peterborough.

Above: 377504 crossing the Ouse Valley Viaduct on 26 May 2014. This, and the many tunnels between Three Bridges and Preston Park, form a bottleneck on the otherwise quadruple track Brighton Main Line.

Left: 377517 is berthed in the dedicated Thameslink sidings at Brighton on 12 September 2014. At that time, Thameslink and Southern were two distinctly separate companies and these sidings allowed Thameslink to have its own Brighton base.

In the 'Core', deep in the heart of London, 377504 calls at Farringdon heading north on 2 May 2014. Farringdon is an important interchange with London Underground services as well as serving the busy Clerkenwell area – it has been made even busier with the recent opening of Crossrail.

Class 387/1s

Due to delays in the new Class 700 fleet for Thameslink, the Department for Transport and Southern ordered 116 electric dual-voltage 110mph carriages (29 units) with the option for another 140 carriages (35 units). The tender for the new Class 387 trains was won by Bombardier, and the first set entered service in December 2014, with all in service by May 2015. By 2018, all units were replaced by the new Class 700 fleet, with the Class 387 fleet moving over to the Great Northern franchise. The units were based at Hornsey depot, but their dual-voltage capability and the fact that they are all currently under the same franchise means it is not unusual to see them at Selhurst depot for maintenance.

These were the first of the Class 387 units to be introduced and had the revised window layout first seen on Class 379s (see Chapter 10).

Right: On test at Redhill, brand-new 387108 heads for Brighton on 25 November 2014. At this time, there were frequent test trips up and down the Brighton line from Bletchley depot, which was being used by Bombardier as a test base, primarily to do 110mph testing on the West Coast Main Line.

Below: Lit by early morning sun at a very cold and frosty Salfords station, Thameslink 387105 runs down the fast lines to Brighton on 31 December 2014.

It seems a long time since Thameslink trains were this short compared to today's Class 700 monoliths. Here we see 387117 waiting to be despatched from Haywards Heath with a train from Brighton on the Midland Main Line, probably to Bedford, on 21 February 2015.

Under the iconic station roof at Brighton, 387114 has just arrived on a service from Bedford on 21 February 2015. It seems, these days, that Thameslink and Gatwick Express have taken over what should be a 'Southern' station, with Southern squeezed out to the periphery.

Chapter 7
Class 387/1s and Class 387/3s Great Northern

387101–387129	DMSO-MSO-PTSO-DMSO	750V dc & 25kV ac
387301–387306	DMSO-MSO-PTSO-DMSO	750V dc & 25kV ac

Regular Routes

Kings Cross–Stevenage–Peterborough
Kings Cross–Cambridge–Ely–Kings Lynn

Partially described in the previous chapter, Class 387/1s are now the staple unit for operating Great Northern services helped with an influx of class 387/3 units. After being displaced from Thameslink services by Class 700s in 2016/2017, the Class 387/1s settled down to service with Great Northern. In 2020, the desire to replace the Class 365 'Networker Express' units from this route was helped by a loan of 387/2 units from sister franchise Gatwick Express, which had become temporarily available thanks to the COVID-19-enforced suspension of the Gatwick Express. In order for some of these to return to

387102 at Peterborough on 14 July 2017. This and King's Lynn are the furthest north that Electrostars reach, which coincidentally are also some of the furthest reaches of Network SouthEast.

their normal operations, Great Northern took on Class 387/3 transferred over from the C2C franchise in 2022. Class 387/3 units can be identified by their blue doors. The Class 387 units have 110mph capability, which is needed on the East Coast Main Line (ECML) to keep out of the way of all the other fast trains on that route.

An important development in late 2022 was the sending of 387101 for fitment of European Train Control System (ETCS), which will allow it to continue to operate on the ECML.

Great Northern, Southern, Thameslink and Gatwick Express are all component parts of Govia, so it is quite reasonable to see Electrostars swapping between routes where speed and electrical supply allow. This also allows a little flexibility in depot usage, and the Hornsey-allocated Class 387/1s are often seen at Selhurst Depot.

Left: 387120 at Gordon Hill on a diversion over the Hertford Loop on 25 February 2018. Electrostars are not normally seen on this route, except when any blockage has occurred between Alexandra Palace and Stevenage on the main line.

Below: 387119 speeding south through Welwyn North and heading for King's Cross on 30 June 2017. The double track here through the two tunnels, which can be seen behind the train and across the viaduct, just south of the station, form the biggest bottleneck at the London end of the East Coast Main Line.

387108 calls at Hitchin on 3 October 2017. This is the junction for trains to Cambridge and King's Lynn, and in recent years a flyover was installed that circumvents the town of Hitchin to avoid conflicting moves north of the station.

387107 at a cold and icy Alexandra Palace on 3 March 2018. This station used to be known as Wood Green but was renamed to reflect the nearby exhibition centre, however it is a very steep walk up the hill to get there!

387125 at King's Cross on 6 March 2018, under the famous train shed and awaiting departure for King's Lynn. This is a fast but long journey, taking around one and three quarter hours.

Speeding down the East Coast Main Line and heading for King's Cross, 387110 passes Welham Green on 13 March 2019. This is where the top speed of 110mph allows the units to run on the mainline.

On a wet and dreary 31 March 2018, 387126 has arrived at Ely on the rear of a train from King's Lynn to King's Cross. In this area north of Cambridge, there has been a boom in house building and industrial development, meaning the railway infrastructure has changed beyond all recognition from that 30 years ago, with a new station opening at Cambridge North and more planned.

On a crisp and cold 15 December 2022, 387126 speeds through Alexandra Palace on a train from King's Lynn to King's Cross.

The King's Lynn line is as far north as Class 387s go, and between the end and Cambridge is Downham Market, where C2C 387306 is calling to pick up passengers on 17 February 2023. Not only does Downham Market ooze Great Eastern Railway character, but it is completely adorned in Network South East regalia as a reminder of that exciting time in railway history.

Chapter 8
Class 387/1s Great Western

387130–387174   DMSO-MSO-PTSO-DMSO   750V dc & 25kV

Regular Routes

Paddington–Reading–Didcot Parkway–Swindon–Cardiff Central
Reading–Newbury

This batch of Class 387/1 units was a direct follow on from the Great Northern units and are almost identical bar some internal seating differences and the livery. The units were purchased in order to provide an outer-suburban service as part of the Great Western Main Line electrification. When the first Great Western Railway (GWR) Class 387/1 units entered service in September 2016, the route was only electrified from Paddington to Heathrow Airport, so the first units terminated at Hayes and Harlington. Progressive electrification extended the route to Didcot Parkway in January 2018, and in January 2019, electrification reached Newbury from Reading. Following electrification to Cardiff, GWR has operated a couple of trains to and from Cardiff Central using pairs of Class 387s.

It is worth noting that 387174 was the last Electrostar constructed. It left Bombardier Derby in November 2017, becoming the last in the line of 2085 vehicles and 18 years of production.

The introduction of class 345 Aventra EMUs to the stopping services between Paddington and Reading by Crossrail allowed 12 of the 387 fleet to be modified to work the Heathrow Express (covered in the next chapter).

Looking very new, 387154 leaves Paddington and passes the Underground station at Royal Oak on 21 August 2017 as it heads for Hayes & Harlington.

387132 calls at Ealing Broadway on 16 September 2017, in the early days of the Hayes & Harlington to Paddington shuttle. This service has now been taken over by Crossrail trains running through the heart of London, but Electrostar trains still call at this important interchange, with the Underground on longer-distance outer suburban trains.

387132 at West Drayton on 6 January 2018. This is just after services started running through to Reading and Didcot Parkway as the Great Western Main Line electrification slowly progressed. The new footbridge and surrounding building works are all part of the upgrades associated with the soon-to-come Crossrail trains.

387155 in the dark at Reading on 15 February 2018, awaiting its return to Paddington.

387155 and 387136 pose at Reading on 17 March 2018, crossing from and to Paddington and Didcot Parkway. Interestingly, and perhaps understandably, these local trains are usually shown as terminating at Ealing Broadway. This encourages potential passengers to use the far faster non-stop Great Western Railway Inter City trains into central London.

387158 stops at Cholsey on a Didcot Parkway to Paddington train on 23 March 2022. An almost original Great Western Railway country station, today it forms the starting point of the Cholsey & Wallingford Railway.

387158 rounding the curve at Pangbourne on a Paddington service on 7 September 2022, working a semi-fast service into Paddington. Logic says these trains should run to and from Oxford, but lack of funding did not allow the wires to be extended the short distance from Didcot, so, for now, this remains the terminus of the outer suburban trains.

The last Electrostar built, 387174, arrives at Reading on 18 May 2019. Its completion marked the end of an 18-year era. The train was running from Paddington to Didcot Parkway, and I am sure that the majority of passengers within did not realise the significance of the train they were riding in!

Chapter 9

Airport Express
Electrostars to Gatwick, Stansted and Heathrow

For a fleet of trains designed primarily for longer-distance commuter routes, it may come as a surprise that they have served four out of five major London airports, three of them with dedicated services. Luton is served by standard Thameslink services, and so the following concentrates on those specific airports with specific express services.

Class 387/2s: Gatwick Express

387201–387227   DMOS-MOC-PTOS-DMOS   750V dc & 25kV

What should be a simple route structure using a dedicated fleet of units has, in fact, become quite complicated thanks to COVID-19 and changing travel patterns. Introduced in February 2016, the 387/2 sub class of 27 units was introduced on the Gatwick Express in order to replace the Class 442s.

The units are maintained at Stewarts Lane and have dual-voltage capability. The pandemic and the resultant reduction of airport passengers effectively temporarily suspended the Gatwick Express service, with the units being used in a common pool. As a result, some were lent to Great Western to help out with the Hitachi Class 800 problems and others were lent to Great Northern to allow replacement of Class 365s, where some still remain.

Resumption of Gatwick Express gradually saw the 387/2s back on their normal route, running fast trains from Victoria to Gatwick Airport and Brighton, with some spare units regularly seen on East Coastway services between Brighton and Hastings. The Class 387/2s add a splash of colour to the Southern network.

387227 heading south to Gatwick Airport and passing Salfords on 16 August 2017.

Above: 387206 passes Earlswood with a service to Brighton on 11 May 2018. The train is passing the disused down fast platform taken out of use with the resignalling project in the mid-1980s.

Right: 387201 approaches Horley on 24 May 2019. This part of the busy four-track Brighton Main Line is fast, although trains must start braking for the stop at Gatwick Airport 2km south.

Speeding through Burgess Hill on a Brighton service is 387227 on 22 October 2020. The Class 73 on the rear of the Network Rail test train can be seen receding into the distance under the bridge.

387219 passes Collington on 3 September 2022, working an Ore to Brighton via Eastbourne train.

387209 running fast through Glynde on another Brighton to Ore via Eastbourne train on 12 September 2022. In the background, one of the original 1935 Southern Railway electric substations can be seen.

387212 leaving Hastings on 18 December 2020 on a Brighton via Eastbourne train. Since the pandemic, these units have been seen on regular East Coastway services.

Class 379s: Stansted Express

379001–379030   DMSO-MSO-PTSO-DMCO   25kV ac

These units exchanged 'ribbon' windows for single side windows, which are easier to replace. These became standard on all subsequent Electrostar units. The units also had a seating arrangement that was more commensurate with an airport express unit, with additional luggage racks and fairly upmarket First Class seating. They were introduced into service in 2011.

The first 20 units were branded as the 'Stansted Express', and the final ten received Greater Anglia branding. These units were intended to be operated on Liverpool Street to Cambridge services, but in practice they became mixed together.

After being replaced by new Stadler units, the Class 379s came off lease in February 2022 and have now been stored awaiting another operator or disposal. This makes them the first Electrostar fleet to be withdrawn and after only 11 years of service.

There was an interesting trial carried out in 2015, in which unit 379013 was fitted with batteries and tested with some success on the Harwich branch. After a couple of months, the trial ended and the unit was converted back to standard.

379004 forms a Stansted Express train passing Hackney Downs in the East End of London on 22 July 2014. The train will shortly arrive at London Liverpool Street.

379011 and 379020 at Liverpool Street on 18 February 2014. In common with other dedicated airport express services, it is usual for at least one unit to be present in a terminal platform for loading purposes so that the airport passengers can board immediately. At this time, Stansted Express trains were operating a 15-minute frequency.

Left: Under a threatening sky, 379005 halts at Tottenham Hale on a Stansted Express service on 18 February 2014. All Stansted Express trains stop at Tottenham Hale to allow easy interchange with the London Underground's Victoria Line.

Below: 379003 cruising through Clapton on 22 July 2014.

379013 is being dragged through Stratford on its way to Derby Works for preparation for the battery EMU trial. Traction is supplied by Network Rail 57310 on 14 May 2014.

Above left: Stansted Express branding on 379011.

Above right: Interior of a Class 379 carriage. To the right, one of the extra luggage racks installed for services on the Gatwick Express can be glimpsed.

379012 at Cambridge on 2 June 2014, having just arrived on a service from Liverpool Street via Bishop's Stortford. Class 379s were used regularly on this service.

Class 387/1as: Heathrow Express

387130–141   DMOS-MOS-PTOS-DMOS   750V dc & 25kV

On 29 December 2020, GWR took over the operation of the Heathrow Express, making Heathrow yet another airport served by Electrostars in a dedicated service. To work the service, the first 12 units of the GWR Electrostar fleet were internally modified to a high standard befitting a premium service and repainted into an attractive silver and purple livery with Heathrow Express branding.

The taking over of a number of local diagrams out of Paddington by Class 345 Crossrail units freed up enough units for Heathrow Express, and the maintenance of the units continues at Reading.

The service runs throughout the day, every 15 minutes, non-stop, from Paddington to Heathrow Airport Terminals 2 and 3, with alternate trains terminating at Terminals 4 or 5. Special fares are charged for this service and the journey time is a nominal 15 minutes.

The units were also fitted with ETCS signalling to work through the airport tunnels and have received the class designation 387/1a.

Above: 387133 speeds past Acton Main Line on 9 December 2022. The Heathrow Express trains normally run on the fast lines out of Paddington, where the 110mph maximum speed can be used to best advantage. The service runs four times per hour and takes 15 minutes to reach terminals 2 and 3 with, a further six minutes to Terminal 5.

Left: 387139 passing Hanwell on 9 December 2022 heading for Paddington. This station is the last in the London area to retain elements of Great Western Railway construction and has been tastefully restored as part of the Crossrail upgrade.

Airport Express

All 12 units dedicated to the Heathrow Express have received names:

387130	San Francisco	387136	Paris
387131	Sydney	387137	Amsterdam
387132	New York	387138	Las Vegas
387133	Tokyo	387139	Dublin
387134	Barcelona	387140	London
387135	Rome	387141	Prague

Right: The nameplates of 387130 and 387138 at Paddington on 9 December 2022.

Below: 387139 passing though West Ealing with a Heathrow Express service on 9 January 2023.

Chapter 10
Off the Beaten Track

The versatility of the Electrostar fleet is proven when units have been lent to cover for a shortage. These are most common to support maintenance requirement or late deliveries of newer units. The following photos illustrate when this has occurred, resulting in different liveries or even classes appearing on unusual routes and services.

Above: Prior to the operation of Class 377/5s on Thameslink services, 377202 was sent north of the river to make full use of its dual-voltage capability for crew training. It is seen at Luton Airport Parkway on such a working, on 4 September 2008.

Left: For a short while in 2009, a 12-car rake of Class 375/9s was lent to Southern by South Eastern to cover a stock shortage. On 21 April, 375924 arrives at Balcombe on a Brighton to Victoria service.

To facilitate 12-car Thameslink trains, a number of Class 377/2s were lent by Southern to First Capital Connect. 377212 is seen at Preston Park on a rainy 8 May 2014.

Right: Clearly showing its '12-car Bubble' branding, 377211 is berthed in the Thameslink sidings at Brighton on 12 September 2014.

Below: For a short while, 378105 worked for Gatwick Express and was adorned with a reverse of the 'normal' Gatwick Express livery, as seen at Gatwick Airport on 9 March 2020.

Southern lent a couple of units to sister company South Eastern, where they were used as part of the common Electrostar fleet. 377164 is leading a Ramsgate to Charing Cross service through Minster on 24 September 2021.

Resulting from a reduction in Gatwick Express services, a number of Class 387/2s were sent over to sister company Great Northern to allow the withdrawal of Class 365 units. 387204 is seen at King's Cross on a King's Lynn service on 19 March 2022.

To cover for a shortage of Hitachi Class 800 high-speed trains, the six C2C Class 387/3 units were loaned to Great Western. 387302 is seen at Reading on a local service to Newbury on 12 April 2022.

Chapter 11
The Future

One thing that seems very uncertain in today's railway industry is certainty. In the normal way of things, the eldest of the Electrostar fleet could be seen to be only halfway through its life at worst. It is 20 years since the first Electrostars hit the rails, and an awful lot has happened since.

While it is clear that classes 375, 377 and 387 have a long future ahead of them, the Class 379s were withdrawn after only 12 years, albeit into storage and awaiting another potential lease. The fact the units are owned by leasing companies that are keen to get a decent return on their investment means that scrapping of units with good life left in them would be a hard pill to swallow. Therefore, it is possible that some of these units might end up working abroad.

Ironically, it seems that the follow-up product from Bombardier (now merged with Alstom), the Aventra, is the greatest risk to the Electrostar. It was the Aventra units that contributed to the demise of Class 379s. C2C is about to take delivery of a small fleet of Aventra units, which could affect some of the Class 357 units if passenger traffic doesn't recover from the pandemic fast enough. Additionally, we have already seen Aventra replace some GWR 387/2 duties as a result of Crossrail. Furthermore, South Eastern put out feelers at the end of 2022 for a new fleet of suburban units, which could have some effect on Class 376s.

One big question is whether examples of Electrostar will be preserved in honour of their contribution to the lives of millions of people around London and the South East? I dearly hope they will be.

Electrostar killer? Crossrail 345016 comes to a halt at Hanwell on a Reading service on 4 December 2018. This would have been an Electrostar diagram a few months earlier.

Other books you might like:

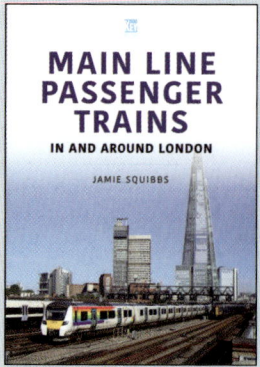

Britain's Railways Series, Vol. 42

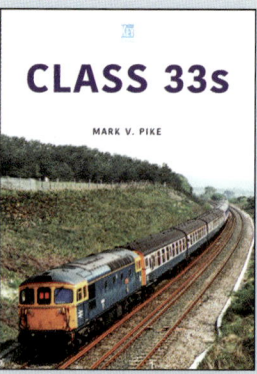

Britain's Railways Series, Vol. 40

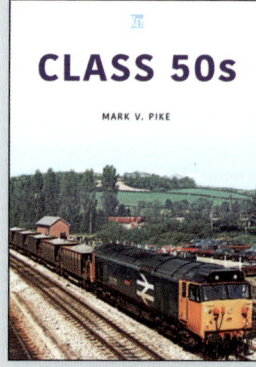

Britain's Railways Series, Vol. 36

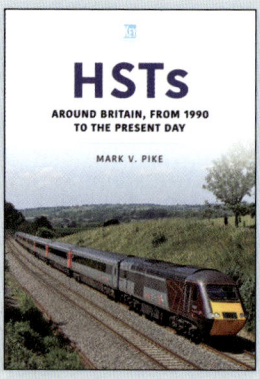

Britain's Railways Series, Vol. 33

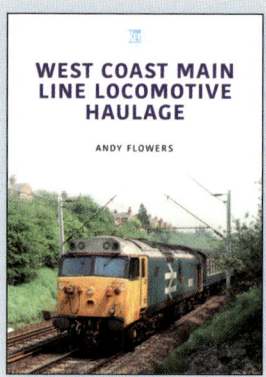

Britain's Railways Series, Vol. 24

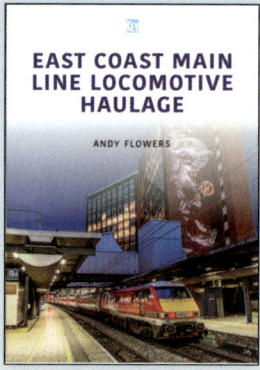

Britain's Railways Series, Vol. 37

For our full range of titles please visit:
shop.keypublishing.com/books

VIP Book Club

Sign up today and receive
TWO FREE E-BOOKS

Be the first to find out about our forthcoming book releases and receive exclusive offers.

Register now at **keypublishing.com/vip-book-club**

Our VIP Book Club is a 100% spam-free zone, and we will never share your email with anyone else. You can read our full privacy policy at: privacy.keypublishing.com